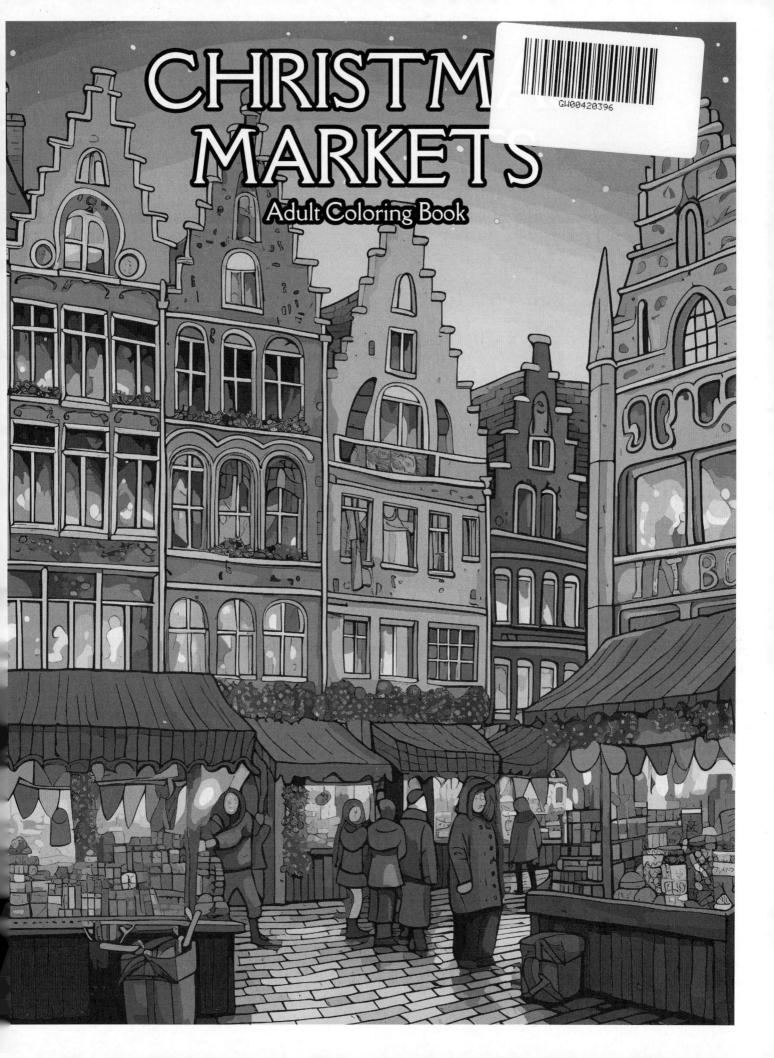

CHRISTMAS MARKETS
Adult Coloring Book

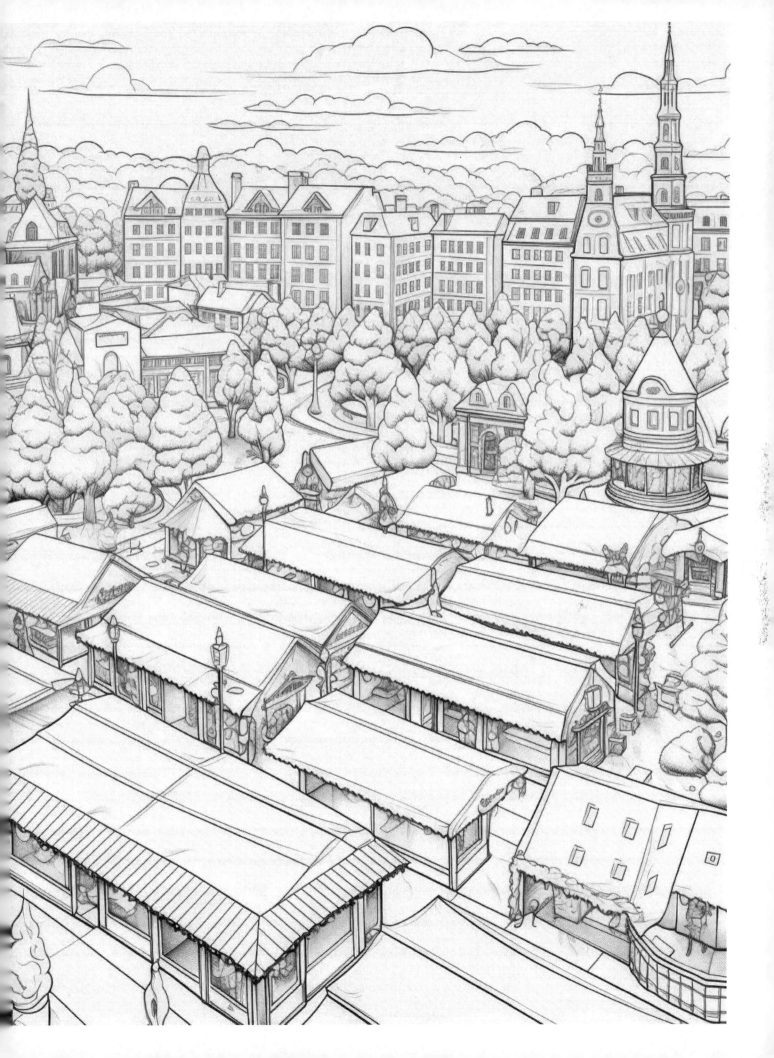

THANK YOU

FOR CHOOSING OUR COLORING BOOK

We would greatly appreciate it if you could take a few moments to share your thoughts and leave a review on Amazon.
Your feedback is important to us and helps us improve our products and services.

Printed in Great Britain
by Amazon

33323696R00046